Kaboom!

PATHFINDER EDITION

By Michael E. Ruane and Beth Geiger

CONTENTS

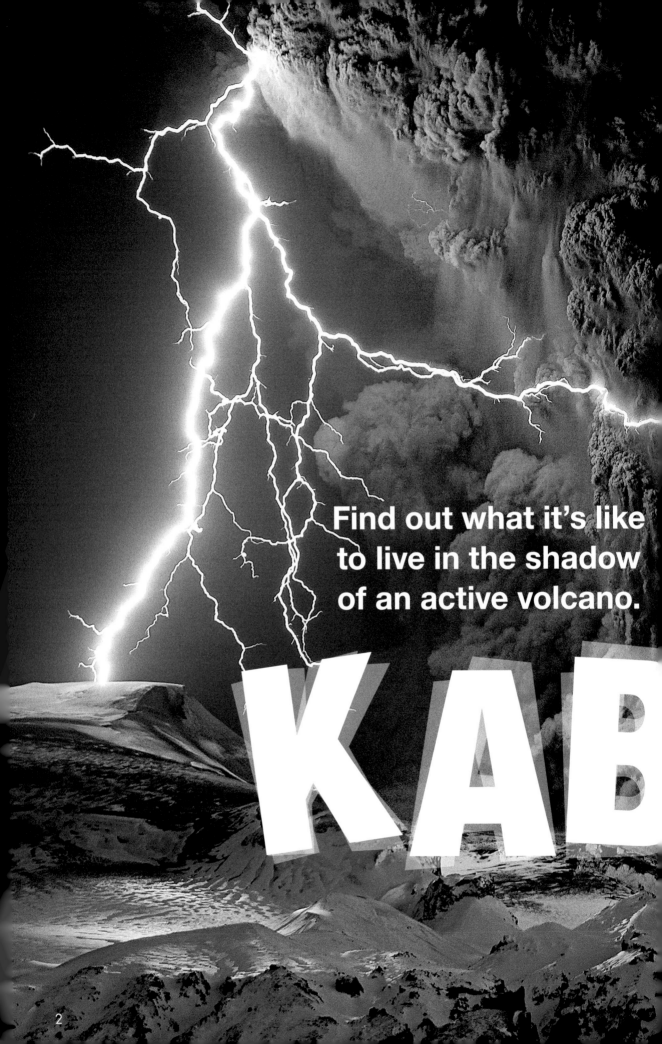

Find out what it's like to live in the shadow of an active volcano.

KAB

OOM!

By Michael E. Ruane

The night was quiet in Iceland, as Hanna Lara Andrews and her family slept peacefully in their little white farmhouse. Suddenly, the phone rang and a government official shouted over the phone, "Get out!"

It was 2 a.m., and the nearby volcano had just erupted.

The family had to hurry; they didn't even have time to be scared. Hanna gathered her one-year-old son and the rest of her family and bolted for the car.

Active Earth

Hanna and her family hadn't worried about the volcano before now, even though it towered over their farm and was only about eight kilometers (five miles) away. They had been raising cows, wheat, and barley on Iceland for years and the volcano had never caused trouble.

Now it spewed a fountain of fire. Ribbons of lava oozed down its steep sides, and **ash** shot toward the sky.

What caused all this action? To understand, it helps to know a little bit about what's going on inside Earth. Let's start with the ground under your feet. It feels solid, doesn't it? Well, it's not solid at all. This outer layer of Earth, called the **crust**, is always moving and shifting.

Deep Heat

Think of Earth's crust as an eggshell. That shell is broken into more than a dozen large pieces called plates, and a layer called the **mantle** lies under the plates. This layer is hot enough to melt some rock and make it flow like molasses. Below the mantle is Earth's core.

The crust's plates float on the mantle. Some bump into each other, and others scrape against each other or pull apart. What exactly is happening beneath Iceland? Here, two plates pull away from each other. Part of Iceland is on one plate, and part of it is on the other.

Volcanoes often rise in places where two plates move apart. This makes a gap where openings can form. A volcano is an opening in Earth's surface that acts as a channel for molten rock, or magma, to reach the surface. Often volcanoes look like mountains.

As the pressure below a volcano builds, magma starts to rise, and when the magma blasts onto Earth's surface, it's called lava.

Lava and Floods

Lava can burn, bury, and destroy everything in its path. Yet when the Iceland volcano erupted, Hanna wasn't worried about the lava. She worried about the flooding. That may seem strange, but here's why.

The Icelandic name of this volcano is Eyjafjallajökull (AY-yah-fyah-lah-YOH-kuul), or Eyja for short. Its name can be broken down into three parts. In English, they mean "island," "mountain," and "**glacier**." That describes Eyja!

A thick glacier covers this volcano and in some places, the ice is 200 meters (650 feet) thick. That's where the eruption began. The extreme heat quickly melted the ice. Hanna feared her farm now stood in the path of a raging river.

Above the Action. *A helicopter flies near the erupting volcano in Iceland.*

Lava Blast. *Lava spurts from Eyja in Iceland in 2010.*

Thin-skinned

If Earth were the size of an apple, the crust would only be about as thick as the apple's skin.

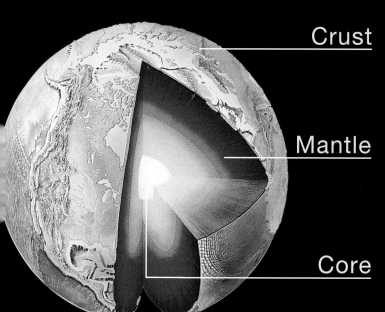

Crust   At its deepest, the crust is only 70 kilometers (43 miles) deep.

Mantle   Magma comes from the mantle, which is 2,900 kilometers (1,800 miles) deep.

Core   The inner core of Earth is solid metal.

Volcano Storm. *Lightning sparks in the ash above Eija.*

Herded to Safety. *Horses are moved away from the volcanic ash.*

A Sleeping Giant Wakes

Seemingly overnight, Eyja had changed into an active volcano. Around the world, as many as 1,500 other volcanoes could become active at any time. Active volcanoes blast out steam, fiery rocks, gases, and ash. People try to stay away from them.

Other volcanoes are extinct, which means they erupted long ago and have stopped for good. If a volcano is not active, but it has not stopped for good, it is called dormant. These volcanoes are said to be "sleeping," and they can be unpredictable and therefore dangerous. Hanna's volcano had been sleeping for a long time. The last time it erupted was in 1821!

This time, it erupted in the middle of the night. With little warning, Hanna and her neighbors had to leave their homes. Even though no one was hurt, many people worried about their homes and farms.

Their animals and crops needed to be cared for, too. Hanna left behind 60 dairy cows. Last time, the volcano spewed for 14 months. Her cows could not wait that long to be milked. What were they going to do?

In the Thick of It

From their safe evacuation spot, Hanna and her neighbors could hear the volcano's deep rumbling sounds, which carried for miles. They also saw spectacular displays of lightning inside the dark cloud of ash.

The lightning flashes when charges of static electricity build up inside a cloud of ash. The same kind of thing happens inside a thundercloud during a storm.

Hearing and seeing the volcano was one thing, but smelling it was quite another. A stinky odor filled the air. Was it rotting seaweed or rotten eggs? The stench burned their noses. When they saw the spreading plume of ash, they understood.

About 24 hours after the eruption began, the ash and foul-smelling gases had risen 11 kilometers (7 miles) into the sky. Air currents carried them over parts of Iceland and beyond. The ash looked like smoke, but it was made up of hard, gritty particles of rock, glass, and sand. It could be fine as talcum powder and dangerous to breathe. Now Hanna and her family had two fears: flooding and ash.

Safe Hiding Place. *Sheep take shelter from the ash cloud. Ash coats their fur.*

Homeward Bound

The floods arrived early the next morning. From her safe position on higher ground, Hanna saw rivers of melted ice spill down the volcano, roads wash out, and homes begin to flood.

Despite the danger, some of Hanna's family headed home. They saw the ash plume sweep across the farmland. Day turned into night as ash blotted out the sun. Their trip was long and difficult, as the ash fell dark and thick, making it hard to see more than a few meters ahead.

Finally, they got there. The farm had been spared! The floods missed it, but some of their neighbors were not so lucky.

For the next several days, they worked hard to take care of the farm. As they worked, they wore masks. They did not want to breathe in the ash. They protected the animals by keeping them in the barn.

It was a great relief that the animals and land were safe, but now Hanna's family had a new problem. Many roads had been washed out by floodwaters. So they had no safe way to get the milk to their customers. They weren't the only people who were stuck. The volcano made it hard for many people to travel.

Faraway Glow. *A woman watches the eruption from a safe distance.*

Buried in Ash. *Volcanic ash covers cars and roads in Iceland.*

Life Interrupted

The ash cloud blew with the winds across the northern part of Europe. Ash is extremely dangerous to jet engines. So airports in England, Ireland, Germany, and France closed, and that left passengers stranded. Some travelers boarded trains, boats, or taxis instead, while many simply waited where they were.

The eruption of one volcano in Iceland caused problems across much of the planet. Supermarkets in Europe couldn't get enough fruits and vegetables, and airmail couldn't cross the Atlantic Ocean. Deliveries of clothing from France didn't arrive in the United States.

Looking Ahead

Time has passed since Hanna and her family fled their home in the middle of the night, and now Eyja appears to be sleeping. Scientists say it has entered a "pause" phase. Lately, only steam and small clouds of ash have risen from it. Life for Hanna and her neighbors is returning to normal. Roads and homes are being repaired.

Still, the people of Iceland remain on edge because Eyja is not Iceland's only volcano. Katla, a more powerful volcano, sits nearby. The last three times Eyja erupted, so did Katla. If that happened again, it could cause even more damage. For now, residents keep a watchful eye on their volcanoes, and people around the world worry about what could happen. They all wait and watch for whatever comes next.

WORDWISE

ash: small pieces of burned material that a volcano shoots into the air

crust: outer layer of Earth

glacier: large mass of moving ice

mantle: layer of Earth under the crust

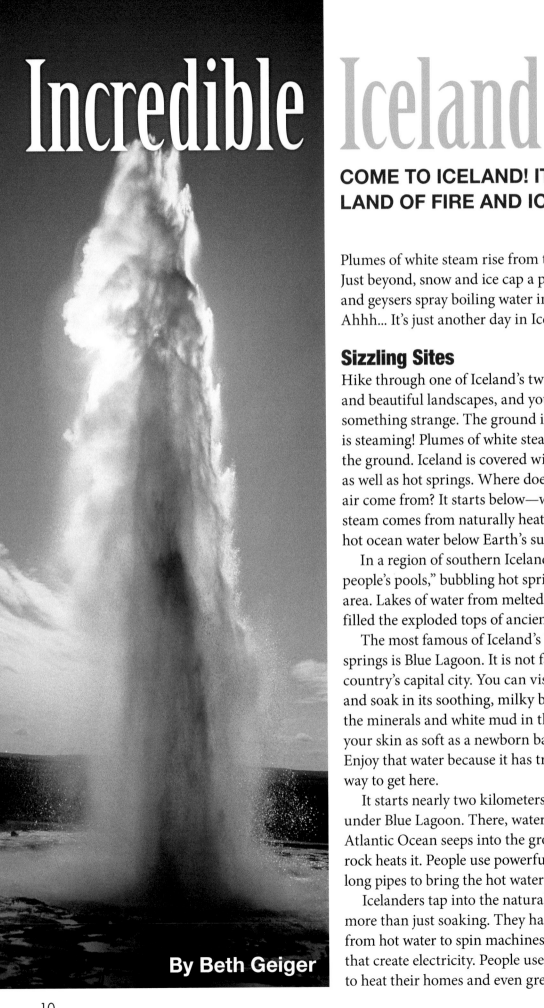

Incredible Iceland

By Beth Geiger

COME TO ICELAND! IT'S THE LAND OF FIRE AND ICE.

Plumes of white steam rise from the ground. Just beyond, snow and ice cap a pink mountain, and geysers spray boiling water in the air. Ahhh... It's just another day in Iceland.

Sizzling Sites

Hike through one of Iceland's twisted, rugged, and beautiful landscapes, and you might notice something strange. The ground in front of you is steaming! Plumes of white steam rise from the ground. Iceland is covered with steam vents as well as hot springs. Where does all the hot air come from? It starts below—way below. The steam comes from naturally heated rocks and hot ocean water below Earth's surface.

In a region of southern Iceland called "the people's pools," bubbling hot springs dot the area. Lakes of water from melted glaciers have filled the exploded tops of ancient volcanoes.

The most famous of Iceland's bubbling hot springs is Blue Lagoon. It is not far from the country's capital city. You can visit the lagoon and soak in its soothing, milky blue water, as the minerals and white mud in the water make your skin as soft as a newborn baby's skin. Enjoy that water because it has traveled a long way to get here.

It starts nearly two kilometers (one mile) under Blue Lagoon. There, water from the Atlantic Ocean seeps into the ground, and hot rock heats it. People use powerful pumps and long pipes to bring the hot water to the surface.

Icelanders tap into the natural hot water for more than just soaking. They harness steam from hot water to spin machines called turbines that create electricity. People use the electricity to heat their homes and even greenhouses.

Meltdown!

What about the ice? After all, Iceland wouldn't be Iceland without ice. One-tenth of the country is covered with glaciers. Imagine one as large as Rhode Island. Glaciers carve the valleys deeper, slowly grinding their way toward the sea.

The largest glaciers are called icecaps. Iceland's biggest one is huge. It's larger than all of mainland Europe's glaciers combined.

Iceland is also one of the few places on Earth where active volcanoes lie below icecaps. Here, fire literally meets ice.

This can make for a dangerous situation. Imagine what happens when a fiery volcano erupts under a glacier. Meltdown! First, the melted water creates a lake hidden beneath the ice. As the lake grows bigger, it eventually runs out of space. It overflows. Then a flood of water bursts out of the icecap.

In 1996, a volcano erupted beneath one of the country's icecaps. The flood that followed was one of the worst Iceland has ever seen. Within hours, the deluge washed away bridges, roads, and power lines.

Extreme Land

Fire and ice meet to create beautiful scenes in Iceland. These sights have a strange and wild beauty. This is a place that's fiery and frozen, strange and spectacular. This is Iceland, a land of fire and ice.

Melted Glacier. *An active volcano under Iceland's largest icecap melted the ice above it and created a lake.*

Bubbling Hot. *These boiling mud pots are made when underground heat mixes clay with steam.*

11

LAND OF
Fire and Ice

Explore Iceland's extremes of hot and cold to answer these questions.

1. Why do volcanoes form where Earth's plates meet?

2. What did the erupting volcano look, sound, and smell like?

3. Why did Hannah worry more about flooding than the erupting lava?

4. How did the ash cloud affect people in Iceland? How did it affect people in other countries?

5. What happens when a volcano erupts under an icecap? List the events in order.